Causes of Acne
p. 47

VIOLENT CRIME

Violent Crime

Homicide, Assault, Rape, Robbery

The Report of the
NATIONAL COMMISSION ON
THE CAUSES AND PREVENTION OF
VIOLENCE

With an introduction:
"Toward a National Urban Policy"
by DANIEL P. MOYNIHAN

George Braziller · New York

Contents

VIOLENT CRIME

Toward a National Urban Policy
Daniel P. Moynihan

IN THE SPRING of 1969, President Nixon met in the Cabinet room with ten mayors of American cities. They were nothing if not a variegated lot, mixing party, religion, race, region in the fine confusion of American politics. They had been chosen to be representative in this respect, and were unrepresentative only in qualities of energy and intelligence that would have set them apart in any company. What was more notable about them, however, was that in the interval between the invitation from the White House and the meeting with the President, four had, in effect, resigned. All but assured of reelection, they had announced they would nonetheless not run again. The Mayor of Detroit who, at the last minute, could not attend, announced *his* resignation in June.

Their decisions were not that uncommon. More and more, for the men charged with governance of our cities

This paper will appear in a forthcoming volume by Daniel P. Moynihan entitled *Toward A National Urban Policy* and is printed here by kind permission of the publisher, *Basic Books*.

great and small, politics has become the art of the impossible. It is not to be wondered that they flee. But we, in a sense, are left behind. And are in trouble. And know it.

At a time of great anxiety—a time which one of the nation's leading news magazines now routinely describes as "the most serious domestic crisis since the Civil War," a time when Richard Rovere, writing of the 1972 elections, adds parenthetically, "assuming that democracy in America survives that long"—these personal decisions may seem of small consequence, yet one suspects they are not. All agree that the tumult of the time arises, in essence, from a crisis of authority. The institutions which shaped conduct and behavior in the past are being challenged, or worse, ignored. It is in the nature of authority, as Robert A. Nisbet continues to remind us, that it is consensual, that it is not coercive. When authority systems collapse they are replaced by power systems, which *are* coercive. Our vocabulary rather fails us here: the term "authority" is an unloved one, with its connotations of authoritarianism, but there appears to be no substitute. Happily, public opinion is not so dependent on political vocabulary, certainly not on the vocabulary of political science, as some assume. For all the ambiguity of the public rhetoric of the moment the desire of the great mass of our people is clear. They sense the advent of a power-based society and they fear it. They seek peace. They look to the restoration of legitimacy, if not in existing institutions, then in new or modified ones. They look for a lessening of violent confrontations at home, and, in great numbers, for an end to war abroad. Concern for personal safety on the part of city dwellers has become a live *political* fact, while the reappearance—what, praise God, did we do to bring this upon ourselves?—of a Stalinoid rhetoric of apocalyptic abuse on the left, and its echoes on the right, have created a public atmosphere of anxiety and portent that would seem to have touched us all. It is with every good reason that the nation gropes for some means to weather the storm of unreason that has broken upon us and seems if anything to grow wilder.

It would also seem that Americans at this moment are much preoccupied with the issue of freedom, or rather with new, meaningful ways in which freedom is seen to be expanded or constrained. We are, for example, beginning to evolve some sense of the meaning of group freedom. This comes after a century of preoccupation with individual rights of a kind which were seen as somehow opposed to and even threatened by group identities and anything so dubious in conception as *group* rights.

The Civil Rights Act of 1964 was the culmination of the political energies generated by that earlier period. The provisions which forbade employers, universities, governments, or whatever to have any knowledge of the race, religion, or national origin of individuals with which they dealt marked in ways the high-water mark of Social Darwinism in America, and did not long stand unopposed. Indeed, by 1965 the Federal government had already, as best one can tell, begun to require ethnic and racial census of its own employees, of federal contractors and research-grant recipients. To do so violated the spirit if not the letter of the Civil Rights Act, with its implicit model of the lone individual locked in equal —and remorseless—competition in the Mancunian market place, but very much in harmony with the emerging

sense of the 1960's that groups have identities and enti-
tlements as well as do individuals. This view is diffusing
rapidly. (In Massachusetts, for example, legislation of
the Civil Rights Act period that declared any public
school with more than 50 percent black pupils to be
racially "imbalanced" and in consequence illegal, is already being challenged—by precisely those who supported it in the first instance.) If, so far, these demands
have been most in evidence among black Americans,
there is not the least reason to doubt that they will now
diffuse to other groups, defined in various ways, and
that new institutions will arise to respond to this new
understanding of the nature of community.

In sum, two tendencies would appear to dominate the
period. The *sense of general community is eroding,* and
with it the authority of existing relationships, while,
simultaneously, a powerful *quest for specific community*
is emerging in the form of ever more intensive asser-
tions of racial and ethnic identities. Although this is
reported in the media largely in terms of black national-
ism, it is just as reasonable to identify emergent attitudes in the "white working class," as part of the same
phenomenon. The singular quality of these tendencies
is that they are at once complementary and opposed.
While the ideas are harmonious, the practices that
would seem to support one interest are typically seen as
opposing the other. Thus, one need not be a moral
philosopher or a social psychologist to see that much of
the "crisis of the cities" arises from the interaction of
these intense new demands, and the relative inability of
the urban social system to respond to them.

Rightly or otherwise—and one is no longer sure of
this—it is our tradition in such circumstances to look to

the condition of government. Social responses to changed social requirements take the form in industrial democracies of changed government policies. This had led, in the present situation, to a reasonably inventive spate of program proposals of the kind the New Deal more or less began, and which flourished most notably in the period between the Presidential elections of 1960 and 1968 when the number of domestic programs of the Federal government increased from 45 to 435. Understandably, however, there has been a diminution of the confidence with which such proposals were formerly regarded. To say the least, there is a certain non-linearity in the relationship between the number of categorical aid programs issuing forth from Washington, and the degree of social satisfaction that ensues.

Hence the issue arises as to whether the demands of the time are not to be met in terms of *policy*, as well as program. It has been said of urban planners that they have been traumatized by the realization that everything relates to everything. But this is so, and the perception of it can provide a powerful analytic tool.

Our problems in the area of social peace and individual or group freedom occur in urban settings. Can it be that our difficulties in coping with these problems originate, in some measure, from the inadequacies of the setting in which they arise? Crime on the streets and campus violence may mark the onset of a native nihilism; but in the first instance they represent nothing more complex than the failure of law enforcement. Black rage and white resistance, Third World separatism, and restricted covenants all may define a collapse in the integuments of the social contract; but, again, in the first instance they represent, for the most part, simply the failure of urban arrangements to meet the expectations of the urban population in the areas of jobs, schools, housing, transportation, public health, administrative responsiveness, and political flexibility. If all these are related, one to the other, and in combination do not seem to be working well, the question arises whether the society ought not to attempt a more coherent response. In a word, ought a national urban crisis be met with something like a national urban policy? Ought not the vast efforts to control the situation of the present, be at least informed by some sense of goals for the future?

The United States does not now have an urban policy. The idea that there might be such is new. So, also, is the Urban Affairs Council, established by President Nixon on January 23, 1969, as the first official act of his administration, to "advise and assist" with respect to urban affairs, specifically "in the development of a national urban policy, having regard both to immediate and to long-range concerns, and to priorities among them."

The central circumstance, as stated, is that America is an urban nation, and has been for half a century.

This is not to say Americans live in *big* cities. They do not. Only slightly more than half (55 percent) of the population lives in cities of 50,000 persons or more, and the bulk of that group is concentrated in relatively small urban aggregations of a hundred thousand to a quarter million persons. Ninety-eight percent of the units of local government have fewer than 50,000 persons. In terms of the 1960 census only somewhat more than a quarter of the Congressmen represented districts in which a majority of residents lived in central-city areas.

The 1970 census will show that the majority of Americans in metropolitan areas, in fact, live in what are known as suburbs, while a great many more live in urban settlements of modest size. But they are not the less urban for that reason, providing conditions of living and problems of government profoundly different from that of the agricultural, small-town past.

The essentials of the present "urban crisis" are simple enough to relate. Until about World War II the growth of the city, as Otto Eckstein argues, was "a logical, economic development." At least it was such in the North Eastern quadrant of the United States, where most urban troubles are supposed to exist. The political jurisdiction of the city more or less defined the area of intensive economic development which more or less defined the area of intensive settlement. Thereafter, economic incentives and social desires combined to produce a fractionating process which made it ever more difficult to collect enough power in any one place to provide the rudiments of effective government. As a result of or as a part of this process, the central area ceased to grow and began to decline. The core began to rot. This most primitive analogue began to suggest to us that in some way life itself was in decline.

Two special circumstances compounded this problem. First, the extraordinary migration of the rural Southern Negro to the northern city. Second, a post-war population explosion (90 million babies were born between 1946 and 1968) which placed immense pressures on municipal services, and drove many whites to the suburbs seeking relief. (Both these influences are now somewhat attenuating, but their effects will be present for at least several decades, and indeed a new baby boom may be in the offing.) As a result, the problems of economic stagnation of the central city became desperately exacerbated by those of racial tension. In the course of the 1960's tension turned into open racial strife.

City governments began to respond to the onset of economic obsolescence and social rigidity a generation or more ago, but they quickly found their fiscal resources strained near to the limit. State governments became involved, and much the same process ensued. Starting in the post-war period, the Federal government itself became increasingly caught up with urban problems. In recent years resources on a fairly considerable scale have flowed from Washington to the cities of the land and will clearly continue.

However, in the evolution of a national urban policy, more is involved than merely the question of national goals and the provision of resources with which to attain them. Too many programs have produced too few results simply to accept a more or less straightforward extrapolation of past and present practices into an oversized but familiar future.

The question of method has become as salient as that of goals themselves. As yet, the Federal government, no more than state or local government, has not found an effective *incentive* system—comparable to profit in private enterprise, prestige in intellectual activity, rank in military organization—whereby to shape the forces at work in urban areas in such a way that urban goals—whatever they may be—are in fact attained. This search for incentives, and the realization that present procedures, such as categorical grant-in-aid programs, do not seem to provide sufficiently powerful ones, must accompany and suffuse the effort to establish goals as such. We must seek not just policy, but policy allied to a vigorous strategy for obtaining results from it.

Finally, the Federal establishment must develop a much heightened sensitivity to its "hidden" urban policies. There is hardly a department or agency of the national government whose programs do not in some way have important consequences for the life of cities, and those who live in them. Frequently—one is tempted to say normally!—the political appointees and career executives concerned do *not* see themselves as involved with, much less responsible for, the urban consequences of their programs and policies. They are, to their minds, simply building highways, guaranteeing mortgages, advancing agriculture, or whatever. No one has made clear to them that they are simultaneously redistributing employment opportunities, segregating neighborhoods, or desegregating them, depopulating the countryside and filling up the slums, and so forth; all these things as second and third order consequences of nominally unrelated programs. Already this institutional *naïveté* has become cause for suspicion; in the future it simply must not be tolerated. Indeed, in the future, a primary mark of competence in a Federal official should be the ability to see the interconnections between programs immediately at hand, and the urban problems that pervade the larger society.

The Fundaments of Urban Policy

It having long been established, that with respect to general codes of behavior eleven precepts are too many, and nine too few, ten points of urban policy may be set forth, scaled roughly to correspond to a combined measure of urgency and importance.

1. The poverty and social isolation of minority groups in central cities is the single most serious problem of the American city today. It must be attacked with urgency, with a greater commitment of resources, than has heretofore been the case, and with programs designed especially for this purpose.

The 1960's have seen enormous economic advances among minority groups, especially Negroes. Outside the South, 37 percent of Negro families earn $8,000 per year or more, that being approximately the national median income. In cities in the largest metropolitan areas, 20 percent of Negro families in 1967 reported family incomes of $10,000 or over. The earnings of *young* married couples are approaching parity with whites.

Nonetheless, certain forms of social disorganization and dependency appear to be increasing among the urban poor. Recently, Conrad Taueber, Associate Director of the Bureau of the Census reported that in the largest metropolitan areas—those with 1 million or more inhabitants, "the number of black families with a woman as head increased by 83 percent since 1960; the number of black families with a man as head increased by only 15 percent during the same period." Disorganization, isolation, and discrimination, seemingly, have led to violence, and this violence has in turn been increasingly politicized by those seeking a "confrontation" with "white" society. Urban policy must have as its first goal the transformation of the urban lower class into a stable community based on dependable and adequate income flows, social equality, and social mobility. Efforts to improve the conditions of life in the present caste-created slums must never take precedence over efforts to enable the slum population to disperse throughout the metropolitan areas involved. Urban policy accepts the reality of ethnic neighborhoods based on choice, but asserts that the active intervention of government is called for to enable free choice to include integrated living as the normal option.

It is impossible to comprehend the situation of the black urban poor without first seeing that they have experienced not merely a major migration in the past generation, but also that they now live in a state almost of demographic seige as a result of population growth. The dependency ratio, in terms of children per thousand adult males, for blacks is nearly twice that for whites, and the gap widened sharply in the 1960's.

CHILDREN PER 1,000 ADULT MALES

	1960	1966
White	1,365	1,406
Negro	1,922	2,216

It is this factor, surely, that accounts for much of the present distress of the black urban slums. At the same time, it is fairly clear that the sharp escalation in the number of births that characterized the past twenty-five years has more or less come to an end. The number of Negro females under age five is exactly the number aged 5 to 9. Thus, the 1980's will see a slackening of the present severe demands on the earning power of adult Negroes, and also on the public institutions that provide services for children. But for the decade immediately ahead, those demands will continue to rise—especially for central-city blacks, whose median age is a little more than 10 years below that for whites—and will clearly have a priority claim on public resources.

1967 NEGRO FEMALE POPULATION

Age	Number
Under 5	1,443,000
5 to 9	1,443,000
10 to 14	1,298,000
15 to 19	1,102,000
20 to 24	840,000

2. Economic and social forces in urban areas are not self-balancing. Imbalances in industry, transportation, housing, social services, and similar elements of urban life frequently tend to become more, rather than less, pronounced, and this tendency is often abetted by public policies. The concept of urban balance may be tentatively set forth: a social condition in which forces tending to produce imbalance induce counterforces that simultaneously admit change while maintaining equilibrium. It must be the constant object of federal officials whose programs affect urban areas—and there are few whose do not—to seek such equilibrium.

The evidence is considerable that many Federal programs have induced sharp imbalances in the "ecology" of urban areas—the highway program, for example, is frequently charged with this, and there is wide agreement that other, specifically city-oriented programs such as urban renewal, have frequently accomplished just the opposite of their nominal objectives. The reasons are increasingly evident. Cities are complex social systems. Interventions that, intentionally or not, affect one component of the system almost invariably affect second, third, and fourth components as well, and these in turn affect the first component, often in ways quite opposite to the direction of the initial intervention. Most Federal urban programs have assumed fairly simple cause and effect relationships which do not exist in the complex real world. Moreover, they have typically been based on "common sense" rather than research in an area where common sense can be notoriously misleading. In the words of Jay W. Forrester, "With a high degree of confidence, we can say that the intuitive solution to the problems of complex social systems will be wrong most of the time."

3. At least part of the relative ineffectiveness of the efforts of urban government to respond to urban problems derives from the fragmented and obsolescent structure of urban government itself. The Federal Government should constantly encourage and provide incentives for the reorganization of local government in response to the reality of metropolitan conditions. The objective of the Federal Government should be that local government be stronger and more effective, more visible, accessible, and meaningful to local inhabitants. To this end, the Federal Government should discourage the creation of paragovernments designed to deal with special problems by evading or avoiding the jurisdiction of established local authorities, and should encourage effective decentralization.

Although the "quality" of local government, especially in large cities, has been seen to improve of late, there appears to have been a decline in the vitality of local political systems, and an almost total disappearance of serious effort to reorganize metropolitan areas into new and more rational governmental jurisdictions.

Federal efforts to recreate ethnic-neighborhood-based community organizations, as in the poverty program, or to induce metropolitan area planning as in various urban development programs, have had a measure of success, but nothing like that hoped for. The middle-class norm of "participation" has diffused downward and outward, so that Federal urban programs now routinely require citizen participation in the planning process and beyond, yet, somehow, this does not seem to have led to more competent communities. In some instances it appears, rather, to have escalated the level of stalemate.

It may be we have not been entirely candid with ourselves in this area. Citizen participation, as Elliott A. Krause has pointed out, is in practice a "bureaucratic ideology," a device whereby public officials induce nonpublic individuals to act in a way the officials desire. Although the putative object may be, indeed almost always is, to improve the lot of the citizen, it is not settled that the actual consequences are anything like that. The ways of the officials, of course, are often not those of the elected representatives of the people, and the "citizens" may become a rope in the tug-of-war between bureaucrat and representative. Especially in a Federal system, "citizen participation" easily becomes a device whereby the far-off Federal bureaucracy acquires a weapon with which to battle the elected officials of local government. Whatever the nominal intent, the normal outcome is Federal support for those who would diminish the legitimacy of local government. But it is not clear that the Federal purposes are typically advanced through this process. To the contrary, an all around diminishment, rather than enhancement of energies seems to occur.

(This would appear especially true when "citizen participation" has in effect meant putting citizens on the payroll. However much they may continue to "protest," the protest acquires a certain hollow ring. Something like this has surely happened to groups seeking to influence public opinion on matters of public policy which have been openly or covertly supported by the Federal Government. This is a new practice in American democracy. It began in the field of foreign affairs, and has now spread to the domestic area. To a quite astonishing degree it will be found that those groups which nominally are pressing for social change and development in the poverty field, for example, are in fact subsidized by Federal funds. This occurs in protean ways— research grants, training contracts, or whatever—and is done with the best of intentions. But, again, with what results is far from clear. Can this development, for example, account for the curious fact that there seems to be so much protest in the streets of the nation, but so little, as it were, in its legislatures? Is it the case, in other words, that the process of public subsidy is subtly debilitating?)

Whatever the truth of this judgment, it is nevertheless clear that a national urban policy must look first to the vitality of the elected governments of the urban areas, and must seek to increase their capacity for independent, effective, and creative action. This suggests an effort to find some way out of the present fragmentation, and a certain restraint on the creation of federally-financed "competitive governments."

Nathan Glazer has made the useful observation that in London and Tokyo comprehensive metropolitan government is combined with a complex system of "subgovernments"—the London Boroughs—representing units of 200,000–250,000 persons. These are "real" governments, with important powers in areas such as education, welfare, and housing. In England, at all events, they are governed through an electoral system involving the national political parties in essentially their national postures. (Indeed, the boroughs make up the basic units of the parties' urban structure.) It may well be, there is need for social inventions of this kind in the great American cities, especially with respect to power over matters such as welfare, education, and housing, which are now subject to intense debates concerning "local control." The demand for "local control" is altogether to be welcomed. In some degree it can be seen to arise from the bureaucratic barbarities of the highway programs of the 1950's, for example. But in the largest degree it reflects the processes of democracy catching up with the content of contemporary government. As government more and more involves itself in matters that very much touch on the lives of individual citizens, those individuals seek a greater voice in the programs concerned. In the hands of ideologues or dimwits this demand can lead to an utter paralysis of government. It has already done so in dozens of urban-development situations. But approached with a measure of sensitivity—and patience—it can lead to a considerable revitalization of urban government.

4. A primary object of federal urban policy must be to restore the fiscal vitality of urban government, with the particular object of ensuring that local governments normally have enough resources on hand, or available, to make local initiative in public affairs a reality.

For all the rise in actual amounts, Federal aid to state and local government has increased only from 12 percent of state-local revenue in 1958 to 17 percent in 1967. Increasingly, state and local governments that try to meet their responsibilities lurch from one fiscal crisis to another. In such circumstances, the capacity for creative local government becomes least in precisely those jurisdictions where it might most be expected. As much as any other single factor, this condition may be judged to account for the malaise of city government, and especially for the reluctance of the more self-sufficient suburbs to associate themselves with the nearly bankrupt central cities. Surviving from one fiscal deadline to another, the central cities commonly adopt policies which only compound their ultimate difficulties. Yet, their options are few. As James Q. Wilson writes, "The great bulk of any city's budget is, in effect, a fixed charge the mayor is powerless to alter more than trivially." The basic equation, as it were, of American political economy is that for each one percent increase in the Gross National Product the income of the Federal Government increases one and one-half percent while the normal income of city governments rises one-half to three-quarters of a point at most. Hence both a clear opportunity and a no less manifest necessity exist for the Federal Government to adopt as a deliberate policy an increase in its aid to urban governments. This should be done, in part through revenue sharing, and in part through an increase in categorical assistance, hopefully in much more consolidated forms than now exist, and through credit assistance.

It may not be expected that this process will occur rapidly. The prospects for an enormous "peace and growth dividend" to follow the cessation of hostilities in Vietnam are far less bright than they were painted. But the fact is that the American Gross National Product grows at better than a billion dollars a week, and we can afford the government we need. This means, among our very first priorities, an increase in the resources available to city governments.

A clear opportunity exists for the Federal Government to adopt as a deliberate policy an increase in its aid to state and local governments in the aftermath of the Vietnam war. Much analysis is in order, but in approximate terms, it may be argued that the present proportion of aid should be about doubled, with the immediate objective that the Federal Government contribution constitute one-third of state and local revenue.

5. Federal urban policy should seek to equalize the provision of public services as among different jurisdictions in metropolitan areas.

Although the standard depiction of the (black) residents of central cities as grossly deprived, with respect to schools and other social services, when compared with their suburban (white) neighbors requires endless qualification, the essential truth is that life for the well-to-do is better than life for the poor, and that these populations tend to be separated by artificial government boundaries within metropolitan areas. (The people in between may live on either side of the boundaries, and are typically overlooked altogether.)

As a minimum, Federal policy should seek a dollar-for-dollar equivalence in the provision of social services having most to do with economic and social opportunity. This includes, at the top of the list, public education and public safety. (Obviously there will always be some relatively small jurisdictions—"the Scarsdale school system"—that spend a great deal more than others, but there can be national or regional norms and no central city should be forced to operate below them.)

Beyond the provision of equal resources lies the troubled and elusive question of equal results. Should equality of educational opportunity extend to equality of educational achievement (as between one group of children and another)? Should equality of police protection extend to equality of criminal victimization? That is to say, should there be not only as many police, but also as few crimes in one area of the city as in another? These are hardly simple questions, but as they are increasingly posed, it is increasingly evident that we shall have to try to find answers.

The area of housing is one of special and immediate urgency. In America, housing is not regarded as a public utility (and a scarce one!) as it is in many of the industrial democracies of Europe, but there can hardly be any remaining doubt that the strong and regular production of housing is very nearly a public necessity. We shall not solve the problem of racial isolation without it. Housing must not only be open, *it must be available.* The process of filtration out from dense center-city slums can only take place if the housing perimeter, as it were, is sufficiently porous. For too long now the production of housing has been a function not of the need for housing as such, but rather of the need to increase or decrease the money supply, or whatever. Somehow a greater regularity of effective demand must be provided the housing industry, and its level of production must be increased.

    6. The federal government must assert a specific interest in the movement of people, displaced by technology or driven by poverty, from rural to urban areas, and also in the movement from densely populated central cities to suburban areas.

Much of the present urban crisis derives from the almost total absence of any provision for an orderly movement of persons off the countryside and into the city. The Federal government made extraordinary, and extraordinarily successful, efforts to provide for the resettlement of Hungarian refugees in the 1950's and Cuban refugees in the 1960's. But almost nothing has been done for Americans driven from their homes by forces no less imperious.

    Rural to urban migration has not stopped, and will not for some time. Increasingly, it is possible to predict where it will occur, and in what time sequence. (In 1968, for example, testing of mechanical tobacco harvesting began on the East Coast and the first mechanical grape pickers were used on the West Coast.) Hence, it is possible to prepare for it, both by training of those who leave, and providing for them where they arrive. Doubtless, the United States will remain a nation of exceptionally mobile persons, but the completely unassisted processes of the past need not continue with respect to the migration of impoverished rural populations. There are increasing indications that the dramatic movement of Negro Americans to central-city areas may be slackening, and that a counter movement to surrounding suburban areas may have begun. This process is to be encouraged in every way, especially by the maintenance of a flexible and open housing market.

But it remains the case, that in the next thirty years we shall add one hundred million persons to our population. Knowing that, it is impossible to have no policy with respect to where they will be located. *For to let nature take its course is a policy.* To consider what might be best for all concerned and to seek to provide it is surely a more acceptable goal.

7. State government has an indispensible role in the management of urban affairs, and must be supported and encouraged by the Federal Government in the performance of this role.

This fact, being all but self-evident, tends to be overlooked. The trend of recent legislative measures, almost invariably prompted by executive initiatives, has been to establish a direct federal-city relationship. States have been bypassed, and doubtless some have used this as an excuse to avoid their responsibilities of providing the legal and governmental conditions under which urban problems can be effectively confronted.

It has, of course, been a tradition of social reform in America that city government is bad and that, if anything, state government is worse. This is neither true as a generalization nor useful as a principle. But on the other hand, by and large, state governments, with an occasional exception such as New York, have *not* involved themselves with urban problems, and are readily enough seen by mayors as the real enemy. But this helps neither. States must become involved. City governments, without exception, are creatures of state governments. City boundaries, jurisdictions, and powers are given and taken away by state governments. It is surely time the Federal establishment sought to lend a sense of coherence and a measure of progressivism to this fundamental process.

The role of state government in urban affairs cannot easily be overlooked; it is more typically *ignored* on political or ideological grounds. By contrast, it is relatively easy to overlook county government, and possibly an even more serious mistake to do so. In a steadily increasing number of metropolitan areas, the county, rather than the original core city, has become the only unit of government that makes any geographical sense; that is to say, the only unit whose boundaries contain most or all of the actual urban settlement. The powers of county government have typically lagged well behind its potential, but it may also be noted that in the few—the very few—instances of urban reorganization to take place since World War II, county government has assumed a principal, even primary role in the new arrangement.

8. The Federal Government must develop and put into practice far more effective incentive systems than now exist, whereby state and local governments, and private interests can be led to achieve the goals of federal programs.

The typical Federal grant-in-aid program provides its recipients with an immediate reward for promising to work toward some specified goal—raising the educational achievement of minority children, providing medical care for the poor, cleaning up the air, reviving the downtown business district—but almost no reward for actually achieving such goals, and rarely any punishment for failing to do so.

It is by now widely agreed that what Federal grant-in-aid programs mostly reward is dissimulation. By and large, the approach of the Federal Government to most urban problems is to provide local institutions with money, in the hope they will perform but with no very powerful incentives to do so.

There is a growing consensus that the Federal Government should provide market competition for public programs, or devise ways to imitate market conditions. In particular, it is increasingly agreed that Federal aid should be given directly to the consumers of the programs concerned—individuals included—thus enabling them to choose among competing suppliers of the goods or services that the program is designed to provide.

Probably no single development would more enliven and energize the role of government in urban affairs than a move from the monopoly-service strategy of the grant-in-aid programs to a market strategy of providing the most reward to those suppliers that survive competition.

In this precise sense, it is evident that Federal programs designed to assist those city-dwelling groups that are least well off, least mobile, and least able to fend for themselves must in many areas move beyond a *services* strategy to an approach that provides inducements to move from a dependent and deficient status to one of independence and sufficiency. Essentially, this is an *income* strategy, based fundamentally on the provision of incentives to increase the earnings and to expand the property base of the poorest groups.

Urban policy should in general be directed to raising the level of political activity and concentrating it in the electoral process. It is, nonetheless, possible and useful to be alert for areas of intense but unproductive political conflict and to devise ways to avoid such conflict through market strategies. Thus, conflicts over "control" of public-education systems have frequently, of late, taken on the aspect of disputes over control of a monopoly, a sole source of a needed good. Clearly, some of the ferocity that ensues can be avoided through free choice arrangements that, in effect, eliminate monopoly control.

If we move in this direction, difficult "minimum standard" regulation problems will almost certainly arise, and must be anticipated. No arrangement meets every need, and a good deal of change is primarily to be justified on grounds that certain systems need change for its own sake. (Small school districts, controlled by locally elected boards may be just the thing for New York City. However, in Phoenix, Arizona, where they have just that, consolidation and centralization would appear to be the desire of educational reformers.) But either way, a measure of market competition can surely improve the provision of public services, much as it has proved an efficient way to obtain various public paraphenalia, from bolt-action rifles to lunar-landing vehicles.

Here, as elsewhere, it is essential to pursue and to

identify the *hidden* urban policies of government. These are nowhere more central to the issue than in the matter of incentives. Thus, for better than half a century now, city governments with the encouragement of state and Federal authorities have been seeking to direct urban investment and development in accordance with principles embodied in zoning codes, and not infrequently in accord with precise city plans. However, during this same time the tax laws have provided the utmost incentive to pursue just the opposite objectives of those incorporated in the codes and the plans. It has, for example, been estimated that returns from land speculation based on zoning-code changes on an average incur half the tax load of returns from investment in physical improvements. Inevitably, energy and capital have diverted *away* from pursuing the plan, *toward* subverting it. It little avails for government to deplore the evasion of its purposes in such areas. Government has in fact established two sets of purposes, and provided vastly greater inducements to pursue the implicit rather than the avowed ones. Until public authorities, and the public itself, learn to be much more alert to these situations, and far more open in discussing and managing them, we must expect the present pattern of self-defeating contradictions to continue.

9. The Federal Government must provide more and better information concerning urban affairs, and should sponsor extensive and sustained research into urban problems.

Much of the social progress of recent years derives from the increasing quality and quantity of government-generated statistics and government-supported research. However, there is general agreement that the time is at hand when a general consolidation is in order, bringing a measure of symmetry to the now widely dispersed (and somewhat uneven) data-collecting and research-supporting activities of the Federal Government. Such consolidation should not be limited to urban problems, but it must surely include attention to urban questions.

The Federal Government should, in particular, recognize that most of the issues that appear most critical just now do so in large measure because they are so little understood. This is, perhaps, especially so with respect to issues of minority-group education, but generally applies to all the truly difficult and elusive issues of the moment. More and better inquiry is called for. In particular, the Federal Government must begin to sponsor longitudinal research designed to follow individual and communal development over long periods of time.

It should also consider providing demographic and economic projections for political subdivisions as a routine service, much as the weather and the economy are forecast. (Thus, Karl Taueber has shown how seemingly unrelated policies of local governments can increase the degree of racial and economic differentiation between political jurisdictions, especially between central cities and suburbs.)

Similarly, the extraordinary inquiry into the educational system begun by the U.S. Office of Education under the direction of James S. Coleman should somehow be established on an ongoing basis. It is now perfectly clear that little is known about the processes whereby publicly provided resources affect educational outcomes. The great mass of those involved in education, and of that portion of the public which interests itself in educational matters, continue, undisturbed, in the old beliefs. But the bases of their beliefs are already thoroughly undermined and the whole structure is likely to collapse in a panic of disillusion and despair, unless something like new knowledge is developed to replace the old. Here again, longitudinal inquiries are essential. And here also, it should be insisted that however little the new understandings may have diffused beyond the academic research centers in which they originated, the American public is accustomed to the idea that understandings do change, and, especially in the field of education, is quite open to experimentation and innovation.

Much of the methodology of social science originated in clinical psychology, and perhaps for that reason tends to be deficiency-oriented. Social scientists raise social problems, the study of which can become a social problem in its own right, if it is never balanced by the identification and analysis of social successes. We are not an unsuccessful country. To the contrary, few societies work as hard at their problems, solve as many, and in the process stumble on more unexpected and fulsome opportunities. The cry of the decent householder, who asks why the profession (and the news media which increasingly follows the profession) must be ever preoccupied with juvenile delinquency and never with "juvenile decency," deserves to be heard. Social science like medical science has been preoccupied with pathology, with pain. A measure of inquiry into the sources of health and pleasure is overdue, and is properly a subject of Federal support.

10. The Federal Government, by its own example, and by incentives, should seek the development of a far heightened sense of the finite resources of the natural environment, and the fundamental importance of aesthetics in successful urban growth.

The process of "uglification" may first have developed in Europe, but as with much else, the technological breakthroughs have taken place in the United States. American cities have grown to be as ugly as they are, not as a consequence of the failure of design, so much as of the success of a certain interaction of economic, technological, and cultural forces. It is economically efficient to exploit the natural resources of land, air, and water by technological means, which the culture does not reject, albeit that the result is an increasingly despoiled, debilitated, and now even dangerous urban environment.

It is not clear how this is to change, and so, the matter which the twenty-second century, say, will almost certainly see as having been the primary urban issue of the twentieth century, is ranked last in the public priorities of the moment. But there *are* signs that the culture is changing, that the frontier sense of a natural environment of unlimited resources, all but impervious to human harm, is being replaced by an acute awareness that serious, possibly irreparable harm is being done to the environment, and that somehow the process must be reversed. This *could* lead to a new, nonexploitive technology, and thence to a new structure of economic incentives.

The Federal establishment is showing signs that this cultural change is affecting its actions, and so do state and city governments. But the process needs to be raised to the level of a conscious pursuit of policy. The quality of the urban environment, a measure deriving from a humane and understanding use of the natural resources, together with the creative use of design in architecture and in the distribution of activities and people must become a proclaimed concern of government. And here the Federal Government can lead. It must seek out its hidden policies. (The design of public-housing projects, for example, surely has had the consequence of manipulating the lives of those who inhabit them. By and large the Federal government set the conditions which have determined the disastrous designs of the past two decades. It is thus responsible for the results, and should force itself to realize that.) And it must be acutely aware of the force of its own example. If scientists (as we are told) in the Manhattan Project were prepared to dismiss the problem of long-lived radioactive wastes as one that could be solved merely by ocean dumping, there are few grounds for amazement that business executives in Detroit for so long manufactured automobiles that emitted poison gases into the atmosphere. Both patterns of decision evolved from the primacy of economic concerns in the context of the exploitation of the natural environment in ways the culture did not forbid. There are, however, increasing signs that we are beginning to change in this respect. We may, before long, evolve into a society in which the understanding of and concern about environmental pollution, and the general uglification of American life, will be both culturally vibrant and politically potent.

Social peace is a primary objective of social policy; to

the extent that this derives from a shared sense of the value and significance of the public places and aesthetic value of the city, the Federal Government has a direct interest in encouraging such qualities.

Daniel J. Elazar has observed that, while Americans have been willing to become urbanized, they have adamantly resisted becoming citified. Yet a measure of this process is needed. There are not half a dozen cities in America whose disappearance would, apart from the inconvenience, cause any real regret. But to lose one of those half-dozen would plunge much of the nation and almost all the immediate inhabitants into genuine grief. Something of value in our lives would have been lost, and we would know it. The difference between those cities that would be missed and those that would not be resides fundamentally in the combination of architectural beauty, social amenity, and cultural vigor that so sets them apart. It has ever been such. To create such a city and to preserve it was the great ideal of the Greek civilization, and it may yet become ours as we step back ever so cautiously from the worship of the nation-state with its barbarous modernity and impotent might. We might well consider the claims for a different life asserted in the oath of the Athenian city-state:

We will ever strive for the ideals and sacred things of the city, both alone and with many;

We will unceasingly seek to quicken the sense of public duty;

We will revere and obey the city's laws;

We will transmit this city not only not less, but greater, better, and more beautiful than it was transmitted to us.

THE REPORT OF THE COMMISSION

Preface

WHEN CITIZENS EXPRESS concern about high levels of violence in the United States, they have in mind a number of different types of events: homicides and assaults, rioting and looting, clashes between demonstrators and police, student seizures of university buildings, violence in the entertainment media, assassinations of national leaders. Foremost in their minds, no doubt, is what appears to be a rising tide of individual acts of violent crime, especially "crime in the streets."

Only a fraction of all crime is violent, of course. Major crimes of violence—homicide, rape, robbery, and assault—represent only 13 percent (or 588,000) of the Federal Bureau of Investigation's Index of reported serious crimes (about 4.5 million in 1968).[1] Moreover, deaths and personal injuries from violent crime cause

---

[1] The FBI Index of Reported Crime classifies seven offenses as "serious crimes"—homicide, forcible rape, robbery, aggravated assault, burglary, larceny of more than $50 and auto theft. It classifies the first four—homicide, rape, robbery, and assault—as "violent crimes" because they involve the doing or threatening of bodily injury.

only a small part of the pain and suffering which we experience: one is five times more likely to die in an auto accident than to be criminally slain, and one hundred times more likely to be injured in a home accident than in a serious assault.

But to suffer deliberate violence is different from experiencing an accident, illness, or other misfortune. In violent crime man becomes a wolf to man, threatening or destroying the personal safety of his victim in a terrifying act. Violent crime (particularly street crime) engenders fear—the deep-seated fear of the hunted in the presence of the hunter. Today this fear is gnawing at the vitals of urban America.

In a recent national survey, half of the women and one-fifth of the men said they were afraid to walk outdoors at night, even near their homes. One-third of American householders keep guns in the hope that they will provide protection against intruders. In some urban neighborhoods, nearly one-third of the residents wish to move because of high rates of crime, and very large numbers have moved for that reason. In fear of crime, bus drivers in many cities do not carry change, cab drivers in some areas are in scarce supply, and some merchants are closing their businesses. Vigilante-like groups have sprung up in some areas.

Fear of crime is destroying some of the basic human freedoms which any society is supposed to safeguard— freedom of movement, freedom from harm, freedom from fear itself. Is there a basis for this fear? Is there an unprecedented increase in violent crime in this country? Who and where are most of the violent criminals and what makes them violent? What can we do to eliminate the causes of that violence?

1

Profile of Violent Crime

BETWEEN 1960 AND 1968, the national rate of criminal homicide per 100,000 population increased 36 percent, the rate of forcible rape 65 percent, of aggravated assault 67 percent, and of robbery 119 percent. These figures are from the *Uniform Crime Reports* published by the Federal Bureau of Investigation. These Reports are the only national indicators we have of crime in America. But, as the FBI recognizes, they must be used with caution.

There is a large gap between the reported rates and the true rates. In 1967 the President's Commission on Law Enforcement and Administration of Justice stated that the true rate of total major violent crime was roughly twice as high as the reported rate.[2] This ratio has probably been a changing one. Decreasing public tolerance of crime is seemingly causing more crimes to

---

[2] Reasons for the gap include failure of citizens to report crimes because they believe police cannot be effective in solving them; others do not want to take the time to report, some do not know how to report, and others fear reprisals.

be reported. Changes in police practices, such as better recording procedures and more intensive patrolling, are causing police statistics to dip deeper into the large well of unreported crime. Hence, some part of the increase in reported rates of violent crime is no doubt due to a fuller disclosure of the violent crimes actually committed.

Moreover, while current rates compare unfavorably, even alarmingly, with those of the 1950's, fragmentary information available indicates that at the beginning of this century there was an upsurge in violent crime which probably equaled today's levels. In 1916, the city of Memphis reported a homicide rate more than seven times its present rate. Studies in Boston, Chicago, and New York during the years of the First World War and the 1920's showed violent-crime rates considerably higher than those evident in the first published national crime statistics in 1933.

Despite all these factors, it is still clear that *significant and disturbing increases in the true rates of homicide and, especially, of assault and robbery have occurred over the last decade.*

While the reported incidence of forcible rape has also increased, reporting difficulties associated with this crime are too great to permit any firm conclusion on the true rate of increase.

Violent crimes are not evenly distributed throughout the nation. Using new data from a Victim-Offender Survey conducted by our staff Task Force on Individual Acts of Violence, standard data from the FBI, and facts from other recent studies, we can sketch a more accurate profile of violent crime in the United States than has hitherto been possible. We note, however, that our information about crime is still unsatisfactory and that many critical details in the profile of violent crime remain obscure. Moreover, we strongly urge all who study this profile to keep two facts constantly in mind. First, violent crime is to be found in all regions of the country, and among all groups of the population—not just in the areas and groups of greatest concentration to which we draw attention. Second, despite heavy concentrations of crime in certain groups, the overwhelming majority of individuals in these groups are law-abiding citizens.

Violent crime in the United States is primarily a phenomenon of large cities. This is a fact of central importance.

The 26 cities with 500,000 or more residents and containing about 17 percent of our total population contribute about 45 percent of the total reported major violent crimes. Six cities with one million or more residents and having 10 percent of our total population contribute 30 percent of the total reported major violent crimes.

Large cities, uniformly, have the highest-reported violent crime levels per unit of population. Smaller cities, suburbs, and rural areas have lower levels. The average rate of major violent offenses in cities of over 250,000 inhabitants is eleven times greater than in rural areas, eight times greater than in suburban areas, and five and one-half times greater than in cities with 50,000 to 100,000 inhabitants.[3]

---

[3] The direct correlation between city size and violent-crime rates may not be as uniform in the South as in other regions. Available data indicate higher suburban violent-crime rates relative to center-city rates in the South, suggesting the possibility that smaller-city

For cities of all sizes, as well as for suburbs and rural areas, there has been a recent upward trend in violent crime; the increase in the city rate has been much more dramatic than that for the other areas and subdivisions. The result in our larger cities is a growing risk of victimization: in Baltimore, the nation's leader in violent crime, the risk of being the victim of a reported violent crime is one in forty-nine per year. Thus, in the context of major violent crimes, the popular phrase "urban crisis" is pregnant with meaning.

Violent crime in the city is overwhelmingly committed by males.

Judgments about overall trends and levels of violent crime, and about variations in violent crime according to city size, can be based upon reported offense data. But conclusions about the sex, age, race, and socioeconomic status of violent offenders can be based only on *arrest* data. Besides the gap previously mentioned between true offense rates and reported offense rates, we must now deal also with the even larger gap between *offenses reported* and *arrests made.* Accordingly, conclusions in these areas must be drawn with extreme care, especially since arrests, as distinguished from convictions, are made by policemen whose decisions in

---

rates may also be higher relative to larger-city rates in the South (although direct evidence on this point is not presently available).

Also, it should be kept in mind that the relationships noted in the text are for cities within certain population ranges (*e.g.,* more than 250,000, 100,000—250,000, etc.), not for individual cities. Thus the five cities with the highest metropolitan violent-crime rates in 1968 —Baltimore, Newark, Washington, San Francisco, and Detroit— had smaller populations than some very large cities with somewhat lower rates of violent crime.

apprehending suspects thus determine the nature of arrest statistics.[4]

In spite of the possibly wide margins of error, however, one fact is clearly indisputable: violent crimes in urban areas are disproportionately caused by male offenders. To the extent that females are involved, they are more likely to commit the more "intimate" violent crimes like homicide than the "street crimes" like robbery. Thus, the 1968 reported male-homicide rate was five times higher than the female rate; the robbery rate twenty times higher.

Violent crime in the city is concentrated especially among youths between the ages of fifteen and twenty-four.

Urban arrest rates for homicide are much higher among the 18–24 age group than among any other; for rape, robbery, and aggravated assault, arrests in the 15–24 age group far outstrip those of any other group. Moreover, it is in these age groups that the greatest increases in all arrest rates have occurred. Surprisingly, however, there have also been dramatic and disturbing increases in arrest rates of the 10–14 age group for two categories—a 300 percent increase in assault between 1958 and 1967, and 200 percent in robbery in the same period.

[4] According to the FBI Uniform Crime Reports, about half of all arrests for serious crimes result in pleas of guilty or convictions: in only 88 percent of all arrests does the prosecutor decide he has sufficient evidence to try the case, and of those cases that are prosecuted, only 62 percent result in a plea of guilty or a conviction, often for a lesser offense than the one originally charged. A wide margin of error thus exists between the making of an arrest and proof that the person arrested has committed an offense.

Violent crime in the city is committed primarily by individuals at the lower end of the occupational scale.

Although there are no regularly collected national data on the socioeconomic status of violent offenders, local studies indicate that poor and uneducated individuals with few employment skills are much more likely to commit serious violence than persons higher on the socioeconomic ladder. A forthcoming University of Pennsylvania study of youthful male offenders in Philadelphia, for example, will show that boys from lower-income areas in the city have delinquency rates for assaultive crimes nearly five times the rates of boys from higher-income areas; delinquency rates for robbery are six times higher.[5] Other studies have found higher involvement in violence by persons at the lower end of the occupational scale. A succession of studies at the University of Pennsylvania, using Philadelphia police data, show that persons ranging from skilled laborers to the unemployed constitute about 90–95 percent of the criminal-homicide offenders, 90 percent of the rape offenders and 92–97 percent of the robbery offenders. A St. Louis study of aggravated assault found that blue-collar workers predominate as offenders. The District of Columbia Crime Commission found more than 40 percent of the major violent-crime offenders to be unemployed.

[5] This is a study of 9,945 males born in 1945 and who lived in Philadelphia at least from age 10 to 18. Of this group, 3,475, or 35 percent, were taken into custody by the police for delinquent offences other than traffic violations. Race, socioeconomic status and many other variables are analyzed in this study, supported by NIMH, to be published shortly by Thorsten Sellin and Marvin E. Wolfgang under the title, *Delinquency in a Birth Cohort.*

Violent crime in the cities stems disproportionately
from the ghetto slum where most Negroes live.

Reported national urban arrest rates are much higher
for Negroes than for whites in all four major violent-
crime categories, ranging from ten or eleven times
higher for assault and rape to sixteen or seventeen times
higher for robbery and homicide.[6] As we shall show,
these differences in urban violent-crime rates are not, in
fact, racial; they are primarily a result of conditions of
life in the ghetto slum. The gap between Negro and
white crime rates can be expected to close as the opportunity gap between Negro and white also closes—a development which has not yet occurred.

The large national urban arrest differentials between
Negroes and whites are also found in the more intensive
Philadelphia study previously cited. Of 10,000 boys
born in 1945, some 50 percent of the three thousand
nonwhites had had at least one police contact by age 18,
compared with 20 percent of the seven thousand
whites. (A police contact means that the subject was
taken into custody for an offense other than a traffic
violation and a report recording his alleged offense was
prepared and retained in police files.) The differences
were most pronounced for the major violent offenses: of
fourteen juveniles who had police contacts for homicide, all were nonwhites; of 44 who had police contacts
for rape, 86 percent were nonwhites and fourteen percent whites; of 193 who had police contacts for robbery, 90 percent were nonwhites and ten percent

[6] Because some police commonly associate violence with Negroes
more than with whites, Negroes may be disproportionately arrested
on suspicion, thus producing a higher reported Negro involvement
in crime than is the true situation.

whites; and of 220 who had police contacts for aggravated assault, 82 percent were nonwhites and 18 percent whites. When the three sets of figures for rape, robbery, and assault are related to the number of nonwhites and whites, respectively, in the total group studied (3,000 vs. 7,000), the differences between the resulting ratios closely reflect the differentials in the national urban arrest rates of nonwhites and whites in the 10–17 age group.

The victims of assaultive violence in the cities generally have the same characteristics as the offenders: victimization rates are generally highest for males, youths, poor persons, and blacks. Robbery victims, however, are very often older whites.

There is a widespread public misconception that most violent crime is committed by black offenders against white victims. This is not true. Our Task Force Victim-Offender Survey covering seventeen cities has confirmed other evidence that serious assaultive violence in the city—homicide, aggravated assault, and rape—is predominantly between white offenders and white victims and black offenders and black victims. The majority of these crimes involves blacks attacking blacks, while most of the remainder involves whites victimizing whites. Indeed, our Survey found that 90 percent of urban homicide, aggravated assaults, and rapes involve victims and offenders of the same race.

In two-thirds of homicides and aggravated assaults in the city, and in three-fifths of the rapes, the victim is a Negro. Rape victims tend strongly to be younger women; the victims of homicide and aggravated assault are usually young males but include a higher proportion of older persons. Nearly four-fifths of homicide victims and two-thirds of the assault victims are male. Generalizing from this data, we may say that the typical victim of a violent assaultive crime is a young Negro male, or in the case of rape, a young Negro woman.

Robbery, on the other hand, is the one major violent crime in the city with a high interracial component: although about 38 percent of robberies in the Survey involve Negro offenders and victims, 45 percent involve Negroes robbing whites—very often young black males robbing somewhat older white males. In three-fifths of all robberies the victim is white, and nearly two-thirds of the time he or she is age 26 or over. Four-fifths of the time the victim is a man.

Data collected by the Crime Commission indicate that victimization rates for violent crimes are much higher in the lower-income groups. This is clearly true for robbery and rape, where persons with incomes under $6,000 were found to be victimized three to five times more often than persons with incomes over $6,000. The same relation held, but less strongly, for aggravated assault, while homicide-victimization rates by income could not be computed under the investigative techniques used.

Unlike robbery, the other violent crimes of homicide, assault and rape tend to be acts of passion among intimates and acquaintances.

The Victim-Offender Survey shows that homicide and assault usually occur between relatives, friends, or acquaintances (about two-thirds to three-fourths of the cases in which the relationship is known). They occur in the home or other indoor locations about 50–60 percent of the time. Rape is more likely to be perpetrated by a stranger (slightly over half of the cases), usually in the home or other indoor location (about two-thirds of the time). By contrast, robbery is usually committed outside (two-thirds of the cases) by a stranger (more than 80 percent of the cases).

The victim, the offender, or both are likely to have been drinking prior to homicide, assault, and rape, and the victim often provokes or otherwise helps precipitate the crime. The ostensible motives in homicide and assault are often relatively trivial, usually involving spontaneous altercations, family quarrels, jealous rages, and the like. The two crimes are similar; there is often no reason to believe that the person guilty of homicide sets out with any more intention to harm than the one who commits an aggravated assault. Except for the seriousness of the final outcomes, the major distinction is that homicides most often involve hand guns while knives are most common in assault.[7]

By far the greatest proportion of all serious violence is committed by repeaters.

While the number of hard-core repeaters is small compared to the number of one-time offenders, the former group has a much higher rate of violence and inflicts considerably more serious injury. In the Philadelphia study, 627 of the 10,000 boys were chronic offenders, having five or more police contacts. Though they represented only 6 percent of the boys in the study, they accounted for 53 percent of the police

---

[7] In another report, this Commission has indicated that gun attacks are fatal in one out of five cases, on the average; knife attacks are fatal in one out of twenty.

contacts for personal attacks—homicide, rape, and assault—and 71 percent of the contacts for robberies.

Offenders arrested for major criminal violence generally have long criminal histories, but these careers are mainly filled with offenses other than the final serious acts. Generally, though there are many exceptions, the more serious the crime committed, the less chance it will be repeated.

Americans generally are no strangers to violent crime.

Although it is impossible to determine accurately how many Americans commit violent crimes each year, the data that is available suggests that the number is substantial, ranging from perhaps 600,000 to 1,200,000— or somewhere between 1 in every 300 and 1 in every 150 persons.[8] Undoubtedly, a far-greater number commit a serious violent crime at some time in their lives. The Philadelphia study found that of about 10,000 boys 35 percent (3,475) were taken into police custody for delinquency, and of the delinquents 10 percent (363)

---

[8] The FBI has reported that in 1968, 588,000 violent crimes occurred. This is about 300 crimes of major violence per each 100,000 Americans. It is generally estimated that only about half of all violent crimes are reported; if this is true, the total number of violent crimes per year is in the range of 1,200,000 or 600 per 100,000 people. These are *offenses*, not *offenders*. Since violent crimes often involve several offenders committing a single crime—particularly among the large number of juvenile offenders—a fair guess might be that twice as many offenders (2,400,000) were involved. But some offenders account for more than one crime per year. If we assume the commission of two crimes per year per offender, the total number of offenders drops back to 1,200,000; if we assume the commission of four crimes per year per offender, the total number of offenders is 600,000. Thus, the number of Americans who commit violent crimes each year appears to be somewhere between these figures—between one in every 150 and one in every 300 Americans. Since children under twelve and adults over 45 commit relatively few crimes, the rate for persons between 12 and 45 is even higher.

were apprehended once or more for a major crime of violence before age eighteen.

A comparison of reported violent-crime rates in this country with those in other modern, stable nations shows the United States to be the clear leader. Our homicide rate is more than twice that of our closest competitor, Finland, and from four to twelve times higher than the rates in a dozen other advanced countries including Japan, Canada, England, and Norway. Similar patterns are found in the rates of other violent crimes: averages computed for the years 1963-1967 show the United States rape rate to be twelve times that of England and Wales and three times that of Canada; our robbery rate is nine times that of England and Wales and double that of Canada; our aggravated-assault rate is double that of England and Wales and eighteen times that of Canada.

2

Causes of Violent Crime

VIOLENT CRIME OCCURS in many places and among all races but we have just shown that it is heavily concentrated in large cities and especially among poor black young men in the ghettoes. We must therefore focus on the conditions of life for the youth of the inner city to find the root causes of a high percentage of violent crime.

Much has been written about inner-city slums where crime and delinquency are bred. Social scientists have analyzed slum conditions and their causal link to crime and violence, writers and artists have dramatized the sordidness and the frustrations of life in the inner cities, and a number of Commissions prior to this one have produced comprehensive reports on this subject.[9] In its

[9] President's Commission on Law Enforcement and Administration of Justice, *The Challenge of Crime in a Free Society* (Washington, D.C.; Government Printing Office, 1967); *Report of the National Advisory Commission on Civil Disorders* (Washington, D.C.; Government Printing Office, 1968); National Commission on Urban Problems, *Building the American City* (Washington, D.C.; Government Printing Office, 1968).

1967 Report, the Crime Commission described the linkage between violent crime and slum conditions in large cities as "one of the most fully documented facts about crime." Referring to numerous studies conducted over a period of years, the Commission found that violent crime, its offenders and its victims are found most often in urban areas characterized by:

> low income
> physical deterioration
> dependency
> racial and ethnic concentrations
> broken homes
> working mothers
> low levels of education and vocational skills
> high unemployment
> high proportions of single males
> overcrowded and substandard housing
> high rates of tuberculosis and infant mortality
> low rates of home ownership or single-family dwellings
> mixed land use
> high population density.[10]

A series of studies by Clifford Shaw and Henry McKay remains the classic investigation of these ecological patterns.[11] Extensive data on the distribution of delinquency among neighborhoods were collected in a number of large American cities, and the results for Chicago have recently been updated to cover the period from 1900 through 1965. Finding uniformly high correlations between delinquency and areas having the characteristics listed above, Shaw and McKay focused on the process of change in the communities studied.

Neighborhoods disrupted by population movements

---

[10] *The Challenge of Crime in a Free Society, op. cit.,* p. 35.
[11] Shaw and McKay, *Juvenile Delinquency and Urban Areas,* (Chicago, 1969).

and social change contained high proportions of delinquents. Although the same central core areas tended to experience social change and high delinquent rates over time, high or low delinquent rates were not permanently associated with any particular ethnic or racial group. The newest immigrant or migrant groups tended to settle initially in the core areas and be responsible for the highest delinquency rates in each city; yet the rates for these groups went down as the groups either moved outward to better areas or achieved a more stable community structure. In Chicago, first the Germans and Irish, then the Poles and Italians, and finally Southern Negroes and Spanish-speaking peoples replaced one another as the newest groups settling in the inner city and producing the highest delinquency rates. Consistent with these findings has been a regular decline in delinquency rates from the innermost to the outermost areas around the centers of each city examined.[12] Crime and delinquency are thus seen as associated with the disorganization and deprivation experienced by new immigrant or migrant groups as they strive to gain a foothold in the economic and social life of the city.

Negroes, however, have not been able, even when they have improved their economic condition, to move freely from the central cities. Therefore, movement of Negroes with higher income has tended merely to extend the ghetto periphery. The Southern Negro migrants who have now been concentrated in the cities for two generations—as well as Negroes who have been living under conditions of urban segregation even

[12] One expert testifying before this Commission reported his finding in Chicago: a person living in the inner city faced a risk each year of 1 in 77 of being assaulted; a risk of only 1 in 2,000 in the better areas of the city, and 1 in 10,000 in the rich suburbs.

longer—have experienced the same disorganizing forces as the earlier European settlers, but there are a number of reasons why the impact of these forces has been more destructive in the case of the Negro. Discrimination by race in housing, employment, and education has been harder to overcome than discrimination based on language or ethnic background. With changes in the economy, there has been less demand for the Negro's unskilled labor than for that of the earlier immigrants. The urban political machines which furthered the political and economic interests of earlier immigrants had declined in power by the time the Negroes arrived in large numbers. The cultural experience which Negroes brought with them from the segregation and discrimination of the rural South was of less utility in the process of adaptation to urban life than was the cultural experience of many of the European immigrants. The net effect of these differences is that urban slums have tended to become *ghetto* slums from which escape has been increasingly difficult.

The National Commission on Urban Problems observed in its Report last year that "one has to see and touch and smell a slum before one appreciates the real urgency of the problem." Some of the urgency comes through, however, even in a simple verbal description of the facts and figures of slum life. Before presenting this description (much of which is drawn from the Reports of the Crime Commission and the Kerner Commission), we emphasize again that many slum residents manage to live peaceful and decent lives despite the conditions that surround them, and that the characterizations which follow are typical only of the ghetto core and those who fall into delinquency. They do not describe all neighborhoods or all residents of the inner city.

The Home. If the slums in the United States were defined strictly on the basis of dilapidated housing, inadequate sanitary facilities, and overcrowding, more than five million families, or one-sixth of the urban population, could be classified as slum inhabitants. To the inner-city child, home is often characterized by a set of rooms shared by a shifting group of relatives and acquaintances, furniture: shabby and sparse, many children in one bed, plumbing in disrepair, plaster falling, roaches and sometimes rats, hallways dark or dimly lighted, stairways littered, air dank and foul.

In such circumstances, home has little holding power for a child, adolescent or young adult. Physically unpleasant and unattractive, it is not a place to bring friends; it is not even very much the reassuring gathering place of one's own family. Indeed, the absence of parental supervision early in the slum child's life is not unusual, a fact partly due to the condition of the home.

The Family. Inner-city families are often large. Many are fatherless, permanently or intermittently; others involve a conflict-ridden marital relationship; in either instance the parents may communicate to their offspring little sense of permanence and few precepts essential to an orderly, peaceful life.

Loosely organized, often with a female focus, many inner-city families bestow upon their children what has been termed "premature autonomy." Their children do not experience adults as being genuinely interested or caring persons. These children may, rather, experience adults as more interested in their own satisfactions than those of their children. Consequently resentment of authority figures, such as policemen and teachers, is not surprising. With a lack of consistent, genuine concern for children who are a burden to them, the parents may vacillate from being unduly permissive to being overly stern. Child-rearing problems are exacerbated where the father is sometimes or frequently absent, intoxicated, or replaced by another man; where coping with everyday life with too little money for the size of the family leaves little time or energy for discipline; or where children have arrived so early and unbidden that parents are too immature to put their child's needs above their personal pleasure.

The seeds of delinquency in young boys are shown, studies suggest,[13] in families where there is an absence of consistent affection from both parents, and where there is lacking consistent parental direction. Identification of the boy with a stable positive male image is difficult when the father is frequently absent, erratic in his behavior, often unemployed, unfair in his discipline, or treated without respect by others. Conversely, studies indicate that a stable integrated family life can do much to counteract powerful external influences that pull young men toward delinquency.[14] If the inner-city family, particularly the ghetto black family, were stronger and more secure, with good family relationships, more of its offspring could avoid criminal behav-

[13] See studies cited in "The Family and Violence," Chapter 9 of *Law and Order Reconsidered*, the Report of this Commission's staff Task Force on Law and Law Enforcement (Washington, D.C.; Government Printing Office, 1969) and in "Juvenile Delinquency and the Family," Appendix L of the Crime Commission's *Task Force Report on Juvenile Delinquency* (Washington, D.C.; Government Printing Office, 1967).

[14] *E.g.*, U.S. Dept. of Labor, Office of Policy Planning and Research, *The Negro Family: The Case for National Action* (Washington, D.C.; Government Printing Office, 1965), pp. 38-40.

ior. However, even where there is a stable family which wishes to avoid the problems of slum-ghetto life, continuing racial discrimination makes it difficult for them to remove themselves and their children from the pernicious influences of the slums.

The Neighborhood. In many center-city alleys are broken bottles and snoring "winos"—homeless, broken men, drunk constantly on cheap wine. Yards, if any, are littered and dirty. Fighting and drunkenness are everyday occurrences. Drug addiction and prostitution are rampant. Living is crowded, often anonymous. Predominantly white store ownership and white police patrols in predominantly black neighborhoods are frequently resented, reviled, and attacked, verbally and physically. Municipal services such as garbage collection, street repairs and utilities maintenance and the like are inadequate and, at times, all but nonexistent.

Many ghetto slum children spend much of their time —when they are not watching television—on the streets of this violent, poverty-stricken world. Frequently, their image of success is not the solid citizen, the responsible, hard-working husband and father. Rather, the "successful" man is the cynical hustler who promotes his own interests by exploiting others— through dope selling, numbers, robbery and other crimes. Exploitation and hustling become a way of life.

The School. The low-income ghetto child lives in a home in which books and other artifacts of intellectual interest are rare. His parents usually are themselves too poorly schooled to give him the help and encouragement he needs. They have not had the time—even had they the knowledge—to teach him basic skills that are routinely acquired by most middle-class youngsters:

telling time, counting, learning the alphabet and colors, using crayons and paper and paint. He is unaccustomed to verbalizing concepts or ideas. Written communication is probably rare in his experience.

The educational system in the slums is generally poorly equipped. Most schools in the slums have outdated and dilapidated buildings, few text and library books, the least-qualified teachers and substitute teachers, the most-overcrowded classrooms, and the least-developed counseling and guidance services. These deficiencies are so acute that the school cannot hold the slum child's interests. To him it is boring, dull, and apparently useless, to be endured for a while and then abandoned.

The school experience often represents the last opportunity to counteract the forces in a child's life that are influencing him toward crime and violence. The public-school program has always been viewed as a major force for the transmission of legitimate values and goals, and some studies have identified a good school experience as a key factor in the development of "good boys out of bad environments." The link between school failure and delinquency is not completely known, but there is evidence that youth who fail in school contribute disproportionately to delinquency. One estimate is that the incidence of delinquency among dropouts is ten times higher than among youths who stay in school.[15]

The Job. Getting a good job is harder than it used to be for those without preparation, for an increasing pro-

[15] See "Violence and Youth," Chapter 14 of the Report of our staff Task Force on Individual Acts of Violence. Thirty-nine percent of Negroes and 23 percent of whites in cities fail to complete four years of high school.

portion of all positions require an even higher level of education and training. To be a Negro, an 18-year-old, a school dropout, a resident of the slums of a large city, is to have many times more chances of being unemployed than a white 18-year-old high school graduate living a few blocks away. Seventy-one percent of all Negro workers are concentrated in the lowest-paying and lowest-skilled occupations. They are the last to be hired. Union practices, particularly in the building trades, have always been unduly restrictive toward new apprentices (except those related to union members), and this exclusionary policy has a major impact on young blacks. The unemployment rate, generally down in the last few years, remains twice as high for nonwhites as for whites; and for black teenagers in central cities in 1968 the unemployment rate was 30 percent, up a third over 1960.

Success in job hunting is dependent on information about available positions. Family and friends in middle-class communities are good sources for obtaining information about employment. In the ghetto, however, information about job openings is limited by restricted contact with the job market. The slum resident is largely confined to his own neighborhood, where there are few new plants and business offices, and, unfortunately, state employment services have been generally ineffective even when used.

Most undereducated youngsters do not choose a job. Rather, they drift into one. Since such jobs rarely meet applicants' aspirations, frustration, typically, results. Some find their way back to school or into a job-training program. Some drift fortuitously among low-paying jobs. Others try crime and, if successful, make it their regular livelihood; others lack aptitude and become failures in the illegal as well as the legal world—habitues of our jails and prisons. And there are those who give up, retreat from conventional society, and search for a better world in the private fantasies induced by drink and drugs.

The realities of the employment problem faced by ghetto Negroes are reflected in the data on family income. Negro family income in the cities is only 68 percent of the median white-family income. One-third of Negro families in cities live on $4,000 a year or less, while only 16 percent of the whites do so.

When poverty, dilapidated housing, high unemployment, poor education, overpopulation, and broken homes are combined, an interrelated complex of powerful criminogenic forces is produced by the ghetto environment. These social forces for crime are intensified by the inferiority-inducing attitudes of the larger American society—attitudes that today view ghetto blacks as being suspended between slavery and the full rights and dignity of free men.

The competitive road to success is accorded great emphasis in American life. Achievement often tends to be measured largely in material terms. Our consumer-oriented culture pressures us to desire goods and services and to feel successful if one obtains them, unsuccessful if one does not. The network of mass communications spreads a culture of consumer desires over a vast audience. Happiness, we are endlessly reminded, is obtaining and having things. Most Americans operate on the premise that in the race to material success all men have an equal chance at the starting line, and that anyone who falls behind has only himself to blame. Yet not all can be at the front of the pack, especially not those who started far behind in the first place. And the race has different rules for different participants.

There are many ways of coping with the frustration of failure. Some take solace in the fact that others are even further behind. Some withdraw entirely from the race: alcohol, drugs, mental illness and even suicide are avenues of escape. Others, especially college youth whose parents have succeeded in the race, experiment with "alternative lifestyles" such as those associated with the hippie phenomenon. In the inner city, where the chances of success are less, many adopt illegal means in the effort to achieve their goals of securing more money and higher status among their peers.

To be a young, poor male; to be undereducated and without means of escape from an oppressive urban environment; to want what the society claims is available (but mostly to others); to see around oneself illegitimate and often violent methods being used to achieve material success; and to observe others using these means with impunity—all this is to be burdened with an enormous set of influences that pull many toward crime and delinquency. To be also a Negro, Mexican, or Puerto Rican American and subject to discrimination and segregation adds considerably to the pull of these other criminogenic forces.

Believing they have no stake in the system, the ghetto young men see little to gain by playing according to society's rules and little to lose by not. They believe the odds against their success by legitimate means are greater than the odds against success by crime. The step to violence is not great, for in an effort to obtain material goods and services beyond those available by legitimate means, lower-class persons without work skills and education resort to crimes for which force or threat of force has a functional utility, especially robbery, the principal street crime.

But the slum ghetto does more than generate frustration that expresses itself in violent acquisitive crime. It also produces a "subculture" within the dominant American middle-class culture in which aggressive violence tends to be accepted as normal in everyday life, not necessarily illicit. In the contemporary American city we find the necessary conditions not only for the birth but also for the accelerated development of violent subcultures, and it is in these settings that most violent aggressive crimes, in fact, occur.[16]

From the perspective of dominant middle-class standards, the motives in most criminal homicides and other assaults—altercations, family quarrels, jealousy—are cheap issues for which people give their lives or suffer serious injury. Similarly, the transient gratifications to be obtained from the rape or the robbery do not seem to warrant the risk of punishment or the burden of guilt that is presumably involved. Yet these events are much more reasonable to those in the ghetto-slum subculture of violence, where a wide range of situations is perceived as justifying violent responses.[17] An alterca-

---

[16] The subculture of violence is not the product of our cities alone: the Thugs of India, the *vedetta barbaricina* in Sardinia, the *mafioso* in Sicily and the Ku Klux Klan, for example, have existed for many years. Nor is violence absent from the established middle-class culture of the majority in our society. It is simply the greater frequency and approval of illegitimate violence that distinguishes the subculture of violence from the dominant cultural pattern.

[17] We are here drawing upon Marvin E. Wolfgang and Franco Ferracuti, *The Subculture of Violence*, London: Tavistock Publications; New York: Barnes and Noble, (1967).

tion with overtones threatening a young man's masculinity, a misunderstanding between husband and
wife, competition for a sexual partner, the need to get
hold of a few dollars—these "trivial" events can readily
elicit a violent response in an environment that accepts
violence as a norm, allows easy access to weapons, is
physically and culturally isolated from the rest of the
wider American community, and has limited social controls—including inadequate law enforcement.

Violence is actually often used to enable a young man
to become a successful member of ghetto society. In the
subculture of violence, proving masculinity may require
frequent rehearsal of the toughness, the exploitation of
women, and the quick aggressive responses that are
characteristic of the lower-class adult male. Those who
engage in subcultural violence are often not burdened
by conscious guilt, because their victims are likely to
belong to the same subculture or to a group they believe
has exploited them. Thus, when victims see their as-
saulters as agents of the same kind of aggression they
themselves represent, violent retaliation is readily
legitimized.

Moreover, if the poor, young, black male is condi-
tioned in the ways of violence by his immediate subculture, he is also under the influence of many forces from
the general, dominant culture. As we have said in
another statement, violence is a pervasive theme in the
mass media. The frequency of violent themes in myriad
forms in the media tends to foster permissive attitudes
toward violence. Much the same can be said about guns
in American society. The highest gun-to-population
ratio in the world, the glorification of guns in our culture, and the television and movie displays of guns by

heroes surely contribute to the scope and extent of urban violence.

Taking all the foregoing facts and circumstances into account, perhaps we should marvel that there is not more violent crime in the cities of our nation.

3

The Rise in Violent Crime

IF, AS WE BELIEVE, the conditions of life for inner-city populations are responsible for the sharp difference in violent-crime rates between these populations and other groups in our society, there remains a puzzling paradox to be considered: Why, we must ask, have urban violent-crime rates increased substantially during the past decade when the conditions that are supposed to cause violent crime have not worsened—have, indeed, generally improved?

The Bureau of the Census, in its latest report on trends in social and economic conditions in metropolitan areas, states that most "indicators of well-being point toward progress in the cities since 1960."[18] Thus, for example, the proportion of blacks in cities who completed high school rose from 43 percent in 1960 to 61 percent in 1968; unemployment rates dropped signifi-

---

[18] U.S. Bureau of the Census, *Current Population Reports,* Series P-23, Special Studies (formerly Technical Studies), No. 27, "Trends in Social and Economic Conditions in Metropolitan Areas," U.S. Government Printing Office, Washington, D.C.; (1969).

cantly between 1960 and 1968; the median income of families living in cities rose by 16 percent between 1959 and 1967 (from $6,720 to $7,813), and the median family income of blacks in cities increased from 61 percent to 68 percent of the median white family income during the same period. Also during the same period the number of persons living below the legally defined poverty level in cities declined from 11.3 million to 8.3 million.

There are some important countertrends. The unemployment rate for blacks, though lower, continued to be about twice that for whites; and, as previously noted, unemployment among black teenagers in cities increased by a third between 1960 and 1968 (to 30 percent, two and one-half times the urban white teenager rate). Moreover, figures indicating a closing of the family income gap between blacks and whites in the 1960's do not reflect a number of critical details, such as the fact that in cities black men who worked the year round in 1967 earned about seven-tenths as much as white workers and that this fraction was unchanged since 1959, or the fact that the "dependency ratio"— the number of children per thousand adult males—for blacks is nearly twice that for whites, and the gap widened sharply in the 1960's.[19] The degree of poverty among the Negro poor in metropolitan areas remained severe, half the families reporting incomes $1,000 or more below the Social Security Administration's poverty budget of $3,335 for a family of four. We also find a significant increase in the number of children growing up in broken homes, especially among Negroes and

---

[19] Also, such closing of the family-income gap, as has occurred, all took place after 1965; for the previous 15 years there was no change. See *Law and Order Reconsidered, op. cit.,* at 103.

lower-income families in the cities. Among Negroes, in the cities in 1968, with incomes below $4,000, only one-fourth of all children were living with both parents, as compared to one-half for white families of the same income level. Significantly, for families with incomes of $10,000 per year, this difference between white and black families disappears.

Whatever may be the correct over-all judgment on the change in inner-city living conditions over the past ten years, it is clear, however, that the change has been less dramatic than the change in violent-crime rates during this period. How is this discrepancy to be explained?

In seeking an acceptable answer, we must keep in mind two qualifications, which to a degree mitigate the seriousness of the discrepancy: First, while, as we have said, serious increases have occurred in major crimes involving violence, these increases are not so dramatic as FBI data suggest. Undoubtedly our crime-reporting system is gradually dipping deeper into the well of previously unreported crime. Second, substantial portions of such increases as have occurred are to some extent attributable to demographic shifts in the population, particularly increases in the young population and increasing urbanization of the population.[20]

Even with these two factors taken into account, however, an important part of the original question remains. Why, if a high percentage of the crime in our cities is caused by factors such as poverty and racial discrimina-

---

[20] Computations set forth in the Report of our staff Task Force on Individual Acts of Violence suggest that 18 percent of the increase in the volume of violent crime between 1950 and 1965 is attributable solely to urbanization, and 12 percent to age redistribution alone.

tion, has it increased in a period of unprecedented prosperity for most Americans and in a time of painfully slow and uneven but genuine progress toward racial equality? These questions are not susceptible to precise scientific answers, but it is possible to offer informed judgments about them. In our considered opinion, the following factors have been significantly operative in the increasing levels of violent crime in the inner cities:

(1) The United States has been changing with bewildering rapidity—scientifically, technologically, socially, and politically. Americans literally are changing how we work, how we live, how we think, how we manage our vast enterprise. Other rapidly changing nations—Israel, Japan, Western European countries—also have experienced rapid rises in crime rates, though at a much lower level than ours. Sociologists and anthropologists have long observed that rapid social change leads to a breakdown of traditional social roles and institutional controls over the behavior of young and old alike—but particularly the young, who, because of the social change, are less likely to be socialized into traditional ways of doing things (and not doing them) and, hence, ineffectively constrained by these traditional ways. This process includes the breakdown in traditional notions of civility, respect for elders and the institutions and patterns of conduct they represent, property rights, ways of settling disputes, relations between the sexes, and many other matters.

With economic and technical progress in the United States has come increased affluence for most—but not all—of the members of our society. This combination of rapid social change and unevenly distributed affluence is devastating. At a time when established ways of doing things, traditions of morality, and attitudes about personal and property rights are changing, rising levels of affluence, interacting with public promises of a better life, and television displays of still more affluence have created expectations that have outstripped reality, particularly among the poor and especially the poor black. Rising income statistics look reassuring until one focuses on the continuing gap between black and white incomes.

We have in this country what has been referred to as a "revolution of rising expectations" born of unprecedented prosperity, changes in the law, wars on poverty, space spectaculars, and a host of other features of contemporary life. But, as one of the research contributions in this Commission's Task Force on Historical and Comparative Perspectives points out,[21] a rapid increase in human expectations followed by obvious failure to meet those expectations has been and continues to be a prescription for violence. Disappointment has manifested itself not only in riots and violent demonstrations—but may also be reflected in the increasing levels of violent crime.

(2) Our agencies of law enforcement have not been strengthened sufficiently to contain the violence that normally accompanies rapid social change and the failure to fulfill human expectations. The criminal-justice process, suffering from an insufficiency of resources and a lack of management, has become less effective as a deterrent to crime and as an instrument for reha-

[21] See Davies, "The J—Curve of Rising and Declining Satisfactions as a Cause of Some Great Revolutions and a Contained Rebellion," in *Violence in America,* the Report of our staff Task Force on Historical and Comparative Perspectives, Washington, D.C.; Government Printing Office (1969).

bilitating those who are apprehended and convicted. As we analyze in other parts of our reports, we are allowing law enforcement to falter, the hand gun census to approach 25 million, and an increasing number of crimes to go unpunished. Every successful crime is an inducement to further crime: it advertises society's inability to enforce generally accepted rules of conduct. Weaknesses of our criminal-justice system have had a multiplier effect upon the rise of violent crime.

(3) Public order in a free society does not and cannot rest solely on applications or threats of force by the authorities. It must also rest on the people's acceptance of the legitimacy of the rule-making institutions of the political and social order and of the rules these institutions make. Persons obey the rules of society when the groups with which they identify approve those who abide by the rules and disapprove those who violate them. Such expressions of approval and disapproval are forthcoming only in the group believes that the rule-making institutions are in fact entitled to rule—that is, are "legitimate." What weakens the legitimacy of social and political institutions contributes to law-breaking, including violent crime.

In recent years a number of forces have converged to weaken the legitimacy of our institutions. We repeat what we have said elsewhere: the spectacle of governors defying court orders, police unlawfully beating demonstrators, looters and rioters going unapprehended and unpunished, and college youth attacking society's rules and values, makes it easier, even more "logical," for disadvantaged young people, whose attachment to law-abiding behavior already is tenuous, to slip into law-breaking behavior when the opportunity presents itself. Too, the pervasive suspicion that personal greed and corruption are prevalent among even the highest public officials has fed the idea among the poor that nearly everyone is "on the take," and that the real crime is getting caught.

The beliefs that some claim to be widely held among poor young ghetto males—that the "system" in the United States is collectively guilty of "white racism" and of prosecuting an "immoral" war in Vietnam—have also tended to impair the moral impact upon them of our nation's institutions and laws and weakened the sense of guilt that otherwise would have restrained the commission of violent crimes against society.

These three factors—disappointments of minorities in the revolution of rising expectations, the weakening of law enforcement, and the loss of institutional legitimacy in the view of many—have had their effects on crime rates throughout our society. It is not surprising, however, that their greatest impact has been in the inner cities, among the young, the poor, the male, the black. It is there that reality most frustrates expectations, that law enforcement provides the least protection, and that the social and political institutions of society serve the needs of the individual least effectively. It is in the inner city that a subculture of violence, already flourishing, is further strengthened by the blockage of aspirations whose fulfillment would lead out of the subculture, by the failure of a criminal-justice system that would deter adherence to undesirable subcultural values, and by the weakness of institutions which would inculcate a competing set of values and attitudes.

4

The Prevention of Violent Crime

FOR THE PAST three decades, the primary concerns of our nation have been (a) the national defense, mutual security, and world peace, (b) the growth of the economy, and, (c) more recently, the conquest of space. These challenges have devoured more than two-thirds of all federal expenditures, approximately one-half of federal, state, and local expenditures. We have staked out vast projects to promote the general domestic welfare and to overcome some of the problems we have here analyzed—but in view of dangerous inflationary trends and an already unprecedented level of federal, state, and local taxation, we have not been able to obtain funds to support such projects in a volume and manner consistent with their lofty aims. The contemporary consequence of this pattern of resource allocation is an enormous deficit of unsatisfied needs and aspirations. Nowhere is this deficit more clearly apparent than in our crime-plagued metropolitan areas, where 65 percent of our people are now living.

In the absence of the massive action that seems to be needed to overcome this deficit, our cities are being misshaped in other ways by actions of more affluent citizens who desire safety for themselves, their families, and their investments. The safety they are getting is not the safety without fear that comes from ameliorating the causes of violent crime; rather it is the precarious safety obtained through individual efforts at self-defense. Thus, the way in which we have so far chosen to deal with the deepening problem of violent crime begins to revise the future shape of our cities. In a few more years, lacking effective public action, this is how these cities will likely look:

—Central business districts in the heart of the city, surrounded by mixed areas of accelerating deterioration, will be partially protected by large numbers of people shopping or working in commercial buildings during daytime hours, plus a substantial police presence, and will be largely deserted except for police patrols during nighttime hours.
—High-rise apartment buildings and residential compounds protected by private guards and security devices will be fortified cells for upper-middle and high-income populations living at prime locations in the city.
—Suburban neighborhoods, geographically far removed from the central city, will be protected mainly by economic homogeneity and by distance from population groups with the highest propensities to commit crimes.
—Lacking a sharp change in federal and state policies, ownership of guns will be almost universal in the suburbs, homes will be fortified by an array of devices from window grills to electronic surveillance equipment, armed citizen volunteers in cars will supplement inadequate police patrols in neighborhoods closer to the central city, and extreme left-wing and right-wing groups will have

tremendous armories of weapons which could be brought into play with or without any provocation.

—High-speed, patrolled expressways will be sanitized corridors connecting safe areas, and private automobiles, taxicabs, and commercial vehicles will be routinely equipped with unbreakable glass, light armor, and other security features. Inside garages or valet parking will be available at safe buildings in or near the central city. Armed guards will "ride shotgun" on all forms of public transportation.

—Streets and residential neighborhoods in the central city will be unsafe in differing degrees, and the ghetto slum neighborhoods will be places of terror with widespread crime, perhaps entirely out of police control during nighttime hours. Armed guards will protect all public facilities such as schools, libraries, and playgrounds in these areas.

—Between the unsafe, deteriorating central city on the one hand and the network of safe, prosperous areas and sanitized corridors on the other, there will be, not unnaturally, intensifying hatred and deepening division. Violence will increase further, and the defensive response of the affluent will become still more elaborate.

Individually and to a considerable extent unintentionally, we are closing ourselves into fortresses when collectively we should be building the great, open, humane city-societies of which we are capable. Public and private action must guarantee safety, security, and justice for every citizen in our metropolitan areas without sacrificing the quality of life and the other values of a free society. If the nation is not in a position to launch a full-scale war on domestic ills, especially urban ills, at this moment, because of the difficulty in freeing ourselves quickly from other obligations, we should now, legally, make the essential commitments and then

carry them out as quickly as funds can be obtained. What do our cities require in order to become safe from violent crime?

They surely require a modern, effective system of criminal justice of the kind we recommended in our statement on "Violence and Law Enforcement." All levels of our criminal justice process are underfunded and most are uncoordinated. Police protection and community relations are poorest in the high-crime slum neighborhoods where they should be the best. Lower courts are impossibly over-burdened and badly managed, while juvenile courts have failed to live up to their original rehabilitative ideal. Correctional institutions are generally the most neglected part of the criminal-justice process. *We reiterate our previous recommendations that we double our national investment in the criminal-justice process, that central offices of criminal justice be created at the metropolitan level, and that complementary private-citizen groups be formed.*

In addition to other long-run solutions that we suggest, other immediate steps must be taken to reduce the opportunity and incentive to commit crimes of violence. The President's Commission on Law Enforcement and Administration of Justice made many suggestions which we endorse. In particular, we emphasize the need for actions such as the following (some of which are new):

—Increased day and night footpatrols of slum ghetto areas by interracial police teams, in order to discourage street crime against both blacks and whites; improved street lighting to deprive criminals of hiding places from which to ambush victims; increase in numbers and use of community neighborhood centers that provide activity so that city streets are not deserted in early evening hours.

—Increased police-community relations activity in slum ghetto areas in order to secure greater understanding of ghetto residents by police, and of police by ghetto residents. Police should be encouraged to establish their residences in the cities in order to be a part of the community which they serve.

—Further experimentation with carefully controlled programs that provide low-cost drugs such as methadone to addicts who register, so that addicts are not compelled to resort to robbery and burglary in order to meet the needs of their addiction; increased education about the dangers of addictives and other drugs in order to reduce their use.

—Identification of specific violence-prone individuals for analysis and treatment in order to reduce the likelihood of repetition; provision of special schools for education of young people with violence-prone histories, special psychiatric services and employment programs for parolees and released offenders with a history of violent criminal acts.[22]

—Concealable hand guns, a common weapon used in violent crimes, must be brought under a system of restrictive licensing, as we have recommended in our earlier statement on firearms.

But safety without fear cannot be secured alone by well-trained police, efficient courts, modern correctional practices, and hand-gun licensing. True security will come only when the vast majority of our citizens voluntarily accept society's rules of conduct as binding on them. Such acceptance will prevail widely among those who enjoy, by legitimate means, the benefits and

---

[22] The Philadelphia cohort study cited above shows that out of the entire Philadelphia population of boys born in 1945 (about 10,000), less than 6 percent had five or more police contacts. Even though the age group from 15–24 includes ten such cohorts, the number of identifiable violence-prone youths in a major city such as Philadelphia is still small enough to be manageable.

pleasures of life to which they believe they are entitled —who have, in short, a satisfactory stake in the system. Today the stake of our impatient urban poor is more substantial than it used to be, but unrealized expectations and needs are massive. To ensure safety in our cities, we must take effective steps toward improving the conditions of life for all the people who live there.

Safety in our cities requires nothing less than progress in reconstructing urban life.

It is not within the purpose or the competence of this Commission to detail specific programs that will contribute to this fundamentally important national goal— the goal of reconstruction of urban life. Such programs must be worked out in the normal functioning of our political processes. Many important ideas have been put forth in the reports of the National Advisory Commission on Civil Disorders, the Urban Problems Commission, the Urban Housing Committee[23] and other groups which have made the city the focal point of their studies. Indeed, as the Urban Problems Commission observed, we already have on the national agenda much of the legislation and the programs needed to do the job. Examples are the Housing Act of 1968, the Juvenile Delinquency Prevention and Control Act, the Civil Rights laws of recent years, the President's welfare reform proposal, and many other existing and proposed enactments.

What we urge, from the standpoint of our concern, is that early and accelerated progress toward the reconstruction of urban life be made if there is to be a remis-

[23] These reports are available for purchase from the Superintendent of Documents, U.S. Government Printing Office, Washington, D.C. 20402.

sion in the cancerous growth of violent crime. The programs and the proposals must be backed by a commitment of resources commensurate with the magnitude and the importance of the goal and with the expectations which have been irreversibly raised by the small start already made.

Dr. Daniel P. Moynihan has recently outlined a ten-point national urban policy that embraces many of the recommendations of earlier Commissions and which this Commission, while not in a position to endorse in detail, believes to merit careful consideration.[24] The essentials of the ten points, together with some enlargements of our own, are as follows:

(1) *The poverty and social isolation of minority groups in central cities is the single most serious problem of the American city today.* In the words of the Kerner Commission, this problem must be attacked by national action that is "compassionate, massive, and sustained, backed by the resources of the most powerful and the richest nation on this earth." We must meet the 1968 Housing Act's goal of a decent home for every American within a decade; we must take more effective steps to realize the goal, first set in the Employment Act of 1946, of a useful job at a reasonable wage for all who are able to work; and we must act on current proposals that the Federal Government pay a basic income to those American families who cannot care for themselves.[25]

[24] Daniel P. Moynihan, "Toward a National Urban Policy," *The Public Interest,* No. 17, Fall 1969, p. 15. Dr. Moynihan has been Executive Director of the President's Urban Affairs Council and is now Counsellor to the President.

[25] The President has recently made such a proposal including a work-incentive formula. A somewhat different proposal has been put forward in a recent report of the President's Commission on Income Maintenance Programs.

(2) *Economic and social forces in urban areas are not self-balancing.* There is evidence that some federal programs, such as the highway program, have produced sharp imbalances in the "ecology" of cities, and that others, such as urban renewal, have sometimes accomplished the opposite of what was intended.[26] A more sophisticated understanding and appreciation of the complexity of the urban social system is required—and this will in turn require the development of new, dependable, and lasting partnerships between government, private industry, social and cultural associations, and organized groups of affected citizens. Without such partnerships even the best-intentioned programs will fail or produce unforeseen disruptive effects.

(3) *At least part of the relative ineffectiveness of the efforts of urban government to respond to urban problems derives from the fragmented and obsolescent structure of urban government itself.* At the present time most of our metropolitan areas are misgoverned by a vast number of smaller, independent local governmental units—yet effective action on certain critical problems such as law enforcement, housing and zoning, and revenue-raising, requires governmental units coterminous with metropolitan

---

[26] "Is the only answer to traffic congestion more and wider roads? Clearly in many localities, it is not. The dislocation of people and businesses, the distortion of land use, the erosion of the real property tax base, and the dollars and cents cost, make this an increasingly unacceptable solution." *Tomorrow's Transportation: New Systems for the Urban Future,* U.S. Dept. of Housing and Urban Development, Washington, D.C.; U.S. Government Printing Office, (1968), p. 18. See also *Urban and Rural America: Policies for Future Growth,* Advisory Commission on Intergovernmental Relations, Washington, D.C.; U.S. Government Printing Office, (1968), pp. 59–60.

areas. At the same time, however, many city governments suffer from being too large to be responsive to citizens, especially disadvantaged groups with special needs for public services and for increased political participation.

A dual strategy for restructuring local governments is thus required. On the one hand, steps must be taken to vest certain functions, such as the power to tax and to zone, in a higher tier of true metropolitan governments, each exercising jurisdiction over an entire metropolitan area. On the other hand, our cities must also develop a lower tier of modular neighborhood political units, operating under the direction of representatives elected by residents of the neighborhood and with the authority to determine some of the policies and to operate, at the neighborhood center, some of the services presently performed by citywide agencies.[27] To provide new insights and new momentum for urban government restructuring, we suggest that the President might profitably convene an Urban Convention of delegates from all the states and major cities, as well as the national government, to advise the nation on the steps that should be taken to increase urban efficiency and accountability through structural changes in local government.

(4) *A primary object of federal urban policy must be*

[27] From the standpoint of reducing violence, needed services which might be provided at the neighborhood level include job counseling and training; family counseling and planning advice; medical and psychiatric care; counseling on alcohol and drugs; citizen's grievance agencies; adult education; preschool training and child care for working mothers; psychological counseling for parents during the formative child rearing years; domestic quarrel teams; suicide prevention units; youth bureaus, including counseling of youth referred for non-police action by local Juvenile Squads and Gang Control Units; and legal advice.

to restore the fiscal vitality of urban government, with the particular object of ensuring that local governments normally have enough resources on hand or available to make local initiative in public affairs a reality. Local governments that try to meet their responsibilities lurch from one fiscal crisis to another. Each one percent rise in the gross national product increases the income of the federal government by one and one-half percent, while the normal income of city governments increases only one-half to three-quarters percent at most. Yet federal aid to state and local governments is only 17 percent of state-local revenue, a figure which should be substantially increased as soon as possible. We also believe it is essential to insure that the cities that are most in need of federal funding will obtain their fair share from the states which receive the federal payments.

The President's revenue-sharing proposal is one way to increase state and local revenues. However, it is limited both in the amounts envisioned and in the way they are proposed to be channeled. As an alternate to federal sharing of its tax revenue, consideration might be given to a plan by which a full credit against federal income taxes would be given for all state and municipal taxes up to some maximum percentage of a taxpayer's income. To prevent encroachment by state governments upon the municipal tax base, separate ceilings could be fixed for state tax credits and for municipal tax credits. Such a tax-credit plan for revenue-sharing would be simple to execute, would channel more funds directly to cities, and would eliminate competition among neighboring states and communities to lower tax rates as a means of attracting businesses and upper-income residents. (5) *Federal urban policy should seek to equalize the provision of public services as among different jurisdictions in metropolitan areas.* This includes, at the top of the list, public education and public safety. Not only are both of these vital parts of the public sector severely underfunded, but the available resources are not equitably distributed between, for example, the inner city and suburban areas. What constitutes an equitable distribution may not be an easy question to answer, but it is at least clear that the kinds of inner city-suburban disparities in educational expenditures and police protection reported by the Kerner Commission are *not* equitable.[28] Federal-aid programs should include standards to insure that equitable allocation policies are maintained.

(6) *The Federal Government must assert a specific interest in the movement of people, displaced by technology or driven by poverty, from rural to urban areas, and also in the movement from densely populated central cities to suburban areas.* Much of the present urban crisis derives from the almost total absence of positive policies to cope with the large-scale migration of Southern Negroes into northern and western cities over the past half century, when the number of Negroes living in cities rose from 2.7 million to 14.8 million. In the next 30 years our metropolitan areas will grow both absolutely and in proportion to the total population as this nation of 200 million persons becomes a nation of 300 million persons. We must do the planning and take the ac-

[28] See *Report of the National Advisory Commission on Civil Disorders, op. cit.,* pp. 161–62, 241.

tions—*e.g.*, maintenance of a flexible and open housing market, creation of "new towns"—that are necessary if future urban growth is to be less productive of social and human problems than has been true of past urban growth.

(7) *State government has an indispensible role in the management of urban affairs, and must be supported and encouraged by the Federal Government in the performance of this role.* City boundaries, jurisdictions and powers are subject to the control of state governments, and the Federal Government must work with state governments to encourage a more progressive, responsible exercise of the state role in this process.

(8) *The Federal Government must develop and put into practice far more effective incentive systems than now exist, whereby state and local governments, private interests too, can be led to achieve the goals of federal programs.* In recent years Congress has enacted legislation under which the Federal Government has funded an increasing number of venturesome programs aimed at broadening the scope of individual opportunity for educational and economic achievements. Under many of these new enactments, grants-in-aid to implement the federal policies in health, education, employment and other areas of human welfare have been given not only to state and local authorities, but also to universities, private industries and a host of specially created nonprofit corporations. Although these grants have been made pursuant to specified standards of performance, the results have often been disappointing, in part because there have been inadequate incentives for suc-

cessful performance and inadequate evaluative mechanisms for determining which specific programs are most efficiently and effectively achieving the federal goals.

It is thus increasingly agreed that the Federal Government should sponsor and subsequently evaluate alternative—in a sense "competing"—approaches to problems whose methods of solution are imperfectly understood, as is increasingly being done in the areas of medical and legal services for the poor and educational assistance for disadvantaged children. Other methods of spurring improvement in the delivery of federally supported services include the provision of incentives to deliver the services at the lowest possible cost (as in current efforts with regard to Medicare), and the granting of the federal assistance directly to the consumers of the programs concerned, thus enabling them to choose among competing suppliers of the goods or services that the program is designed to provide (as in the GI Bill and other federal scholarship programs).

(9) *The Federal Government must provide more and better information concerning urban affairs, and should sponsor extensive and sustained research into urban problems.* Social-science research is increasingly able to supply policy-makers and the public with empirical indicators of the nature of social problems and the success or failure of efforts to solve these problems. The time is at hand when these indicators should be systematically collected and disseminated in aid of public policy at all levels.

(10) *The Federal Government, by its own example, and by incentives, should seek the development of a*

far-heightened sense of the finite resources of the natural environment, and the fundamental importance of aesthetics in successful urban growth. Many American cities have grown to be ugly and inhumane largely because of an unrestrained technological exploitation of the resources of land, air, and water by the economically most efficient means. That there has been too little restraint is not suprising in view of the over-all American cultural context in which the natural environment was perceived as an inexhaustible frontier impervious to human harm. Today, however, the critical cultural context seems to be changing, and the "frontier spirit" is giving way to a new conservation ethic more appropriate to a crowded urban society. Government should take the lead in encouraging, and in acting consistently with, the development of this new ethic.

5

Conclusion

TO SUMMARIZE, Our basic findings:

—Violent crimes are chiefly a problem of the cities of the nation, and there violent crimes are committed mainly by the young, poor, male inhabitants of the ghetto slum.

—In the slums increasingly powerful social forces are generating rising levels of violent crime which, unless checked, threaten to turn our cities into defensive, fearful societies.

—An improved criminal-justice system is required to contain the growth of violent crime, but only progress toward urban reconstruction can reduce the strength of the crime-causing forces in the inner city and thus reverse the direction of present crime trends.

Our confidence in the correctness of these findings is strengthened by the support of the findings of the President's Commission on Law Enforcement and Administration of Justice and by subsequent events. At the end of its monumental work, in February of 1967, that Commission not only called for scores of improvements in the effectiveness and fairness of the law-enforcement process, it also identified the same basic causes of violent crime and said this about their cure:

"Warring on poverty, inadequate housing and unemployment, is warring on crime. A civil rights law is a law against crime. Money for schools is money against crime. Medical, psychiatric, and family-counseling services are services against crime. More broadly and most importantly every effort to improve life in America's 'inner cities' is an effort against crime."

National Commission on the Causes and Prevention of Violence

Members of the Commission

DR. MILTON S. EISENHOWER, *Chairman*
JUDGE A. LEON HIGGINBOTHAM, *Vice Chairman*
CONGRESSMAN HALE BOGGS
TERENCE CARDINAL COOKE
AMBASSADOR PATRICIA ROBERTS HARRIS
SENATOR PHILIP A. HART
ERIC HOFFER
SENATOR ROMAN HRUSKA
LEON JAWORSKI
ALBERT E. JENNER, JR.
CONGRESSMAN WILLIAM M. McCULLOCH
JUDGE ERNEST W. McFARLAND
DR. W. WALTER MENNINGER

Staff Officers of the Commission

LLOYD N. CUTLER, *Executive Director*
THOMAS D. BARR, *Deputy Director*
JAMES F. SHORT, JR. and MARVIN E. WOLFGANG,
       Co-Directors of Research
JAMES S. CAMPBELL, *General Counsel*
WILLIAM G. McDONALD, *Administrative Officer*
JOSEPH LAITIN, *Director of Information*
RONALD WOLK, *Special Assistant to the Chairman*